What Would You Do?

GEORGE WASHINGTON CROSSES THE DELAWARE

Would You Risk the Revolution?

Elaine Landau

Enslow Elementary

an imprint of

Enslow Publishers, Inc.
40 Industrial Road
Box 398
Berkeley Heights, NJ 07922
USA

http://www.enslow.com

Enslow Elementary, an imprint of Enslow Publishers, Inc.

Enslow Elementary® is a registered trademark of Enslow Publishers, Inc.

Library of Congress Cataloging-in-Publication Data

Landau, Elaine.
  George Washington crosses the Delaware : would you risk the Revolution? / Elaine Landau.
    p. cm. — (What would you do?)
  Summary: "A basic introduction to George Washington's crossing of the Delaware River during the American Revolutionary War, and the Continental Army's victories at Trenton and Princeton"—Provided by publisher.
  Includes index.
  ISBN-13: 978-0-7660-2904-0
  ISBN-10: 0-7660-2904-2
  1. Trenton, Battle of, Trenton, N.J., 1776—Juvenile literature. 2. Princeton, Battle of, Princeton, N.J., 1777—Juvenile literature. 3. Washington, George, 1732–1799—Military leadership—Juvenile literature. I. Title.
  E241.T7L36 2008
  973.3'32—dc22

                                    2007044882

Printed in the United States of America

To Our Readers:
We have done our best to make sure all Internet Addresses in this book were active and appropriate when we went to press. However, the author and the publisher have no control over and assume no liability for the material available on those Internet sites or on other Web sites they may link to. Any comments or suggestions can be sent by e-mail to comments@enslow.com or to the address on the back cover.

Every effort has been made to locate all copyright holders of material used in this book. If any errors or omissions have occurred, corrections will be made in future editions of this book.

♻ Enslow Publishers, Inc., is committed to printing our books on recycled paper. The paper in every book contains 10% to 30% post-consumer waste (PCW). The cover board on the outside of each book contains 100% PCW. Our goal is to do our part to help young people and the environment too!

CONTENTS

COLD AND HUNGRY SOLDIERS

It was a cold December night in 1776. American soldiers sat shivering at their camp in Pennsylvania. They longed for a good hot meal and warm clothes. Instead, they wore tattered jackets and were hungry.

Yet there was no turning back. These soldiers were American colonists. They were fighting Britain for their freedom. If they won, the colonies would become an independent nation.

Two members of the Continental Army march in the winter. They are playing music to help the soldiers march.

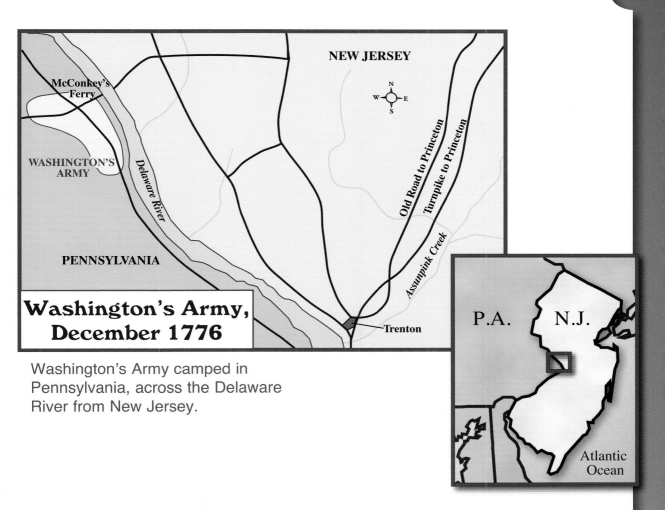

Washington's Army, December 1776

Washington's Army camped in Pennsylvania, across the Delaware River from New Jersey.

However, things were not going well. The British had captured both Boston and New York. It looked like Britain might win the war.

George Washington was in charge of the colonists' fighting force. It was called the Continental Army. Washington knew that his army was in trouble.

The Americans had fought bravely at Bunker Hill in Boston. However, the British still ended up capturing the city.

The British had chased them across New Jersey and into Pennsylvania. Now they were camped near the banks of the Delaware River. Washington needed more soldiers to win the war.

That meant sending out some men to recruit them. Yet sending a small group of soldiers off on their own was risky. What if the British attacked before his men got back? Washington was sure they would be defeated.

Still, without more men, winning seemed unlikely.

WHAT WOULD YOU DO?

What if you were George Washington? *Would you . . .*

* ✳ **Send the men out? Maybe they will bring back a large number of recruits.**

* ✳ **Do the best you can with the men you have? Everyone will just have to fight harder.**

* ✳ **Spread the word that more men are needed? Perhaps some men will join up on their own.**

General George Washington

MEN LOOK FOR RECRUITS TO FIGHT THE BRITISH

Washington sent a few soldiers to find people to join the army. Luckily, they soon returned with a good number of

recruits. Winning the war would still not be easy. The British were just across the Delaware River in New Jersey.

British General William Howe was in charge there. Howe was also short of men. However, he still wanted to control the whole state. Then the British

General William Howe led the British troops in New Jersey.

This uniform was worn by a British officer during the Revolutionary War.

would have won much of the northern colonies.

Howe would have to scatter his forces throughout New Jersey. There would only be a small number of troops in each place. That could be dangerous. What if Washington's men attacked? There would not be a large enough force in any one town to defeat them.

Despite his lack of men, Howe felt safe. He did not think Washington would strike. He believed that the Continental Army was too hurt to make a move.

The hard winter had taken its toll on Washington's army (above). British General William Howe hoped that this would keep the Americans from attacking. Even today the Delaware River (right) becomes choked with ice in the winter. Chunks of ice like these were what Washington and his soldiers faced in 1776 if they wanted to cross the river.

Besides, Washington would have to cross the Delaware. That would be hard to do in the winter. The water was filled with large chunks of floating ice.

Washington's men could not march across the river because it was not frozen solid. Getting their boats across would be difficult, too. However, General Howe knew that difficult was not the same as impossible. There was always a chance that Washington could get his men across.

WHAT WOULD YOU DO?

What if you were General Howe? *Would you . . .*

✳ **Spread your forces throughout the state?**

✳ **Play it safe and keep all your forces where they are?**

✳ **Send for more British soldiers from another area to help your men?**

HOWE SCATTERS HIS MEN

General Howe sent his men to different parts of New Jersey. Now there were British soldiers nearly everywhere. There were just not too many of them in any one place.

The British were not fighting the war alone. They had hired Hessian soldiers to help them. Howe had placed these soldiers all along the Delaware.

British soldiers (at right) fought alongside Hessian soldiers (at left) during the Revolutionary War.

Hessian soldiers often wore green uniforms. They fought the American rebels throughout the war.

This plate was used to cover a Hessian soldier's cartridge box. A cartridge held the ammunition for a soldier's gun.

But because of this decision, many of the Hessians did not feel very safe from enemy attacks. This fact was especially true for the men guarding the area along the Delaware River.

Hessian Colonel Johann Rall was in charge at Trenton. That was the New Jersey town across the river from Washington's camp. Having the American soldiers so close worried some of Rall's officers.

They felt that Trenton was too easy to attack. They urged Rall to build a barricade along the Delaware. But Rall was not sure they needed it. He had seen how easily the Continental Army had been defeated in the past.

Besides, Rall did not think they would be at Trenton very long. He wanted to cross the Delaware River and capture Philadelphia. That was the most important city in the colonies. The colonists' government, called the Continental Congress, worked there.

WHAT WOULD YOU DO?

What if you were Colonel Rall? *Would you . . .*

* ✳ **Listen to your men? Build a barricade along the Delaware River.**

* ✳ **Do nothing? Washington's army is probably too weak to attack anyway.**

* ✳ **Attack Washington's soldiers? It is better to defeat them before they try to cross the river.**

RALL DOES NOT ATTACK

Colonel Rall could not attack Washington's camp. The Continental Army had taken all the boats when it had crossed the Delaware River. For now, the Hessians had no way to get across the river to attack.

James Ewing was one of the very best colonial officers. Ewing was in charge of about six hundred men posted at Ferry Station. That was across from a Hessian

James Ewing was stationed near this ferry house in Pennsylvania. Washington later used the house to meet with his officers.

16

Ewing's soldiers loaded their muskets for a daring raid on the British. Here, an actor in a colonial uniform shows how this was done.

outpost at Trenton. A small group of Hessian soldiers were on duty at the outpost.

Ewing was only told to guard the river. But he did much more than that. He raided the enemy's camp.

A raid took place on December 17, 1776. Ewing and thirty of his men crossed the river in small boats. They struck like lightning. His men stormed the Hessian outpost, firing full blast

Hessian soldiers wore pointed caps into battle. This cap was found in Red Bank, New Jersey, near the site of Fort Mercer.

at the stunned enemy soldiers. Ewing's men left the Hessians dazed in a cloud of gun smoke.

The attack shocked Colonel Rall. He had not expected such bravery from the Americans.

Rall put more men at the outpost. He wanted to be ready if Ewing and his troops struck again.

Ewing and his men attacked the very next morning, on December 18. This time they attacked the Hessians even more fiercely. Several Hessian soldiers were killed. Some were wounded as well. The Hessians fired back, but Ewing's men were too quick for them. They left unharmed.

After that, Rall stayed ready for Ewing. He posted all his men at the outpost. He put two cannons there as well. However, Ewing did not turn up again.

Rall's men remained on guard there. Yet now, they could not gather in large groups anymore. Ewing pointed

Ewing used his cannons to fire on the Hessians from across the river.

thirty cannons at them from across the river. Whenever the Hessians stood together, Ewing's men fired on them.

The Hessians were exhausted. Their spirits were low. Ewing's raids had worn them out.

WHAT WOULD YOU DO?

What if you were James Ewing? Your daytime raids have worked well. *Would you . . .*

* **Dare stage a nighttime raid? That would really catch the Hessians off guard!**

* **Stop now? If you attack again, you could lose.**

EWING STRIKES AT NIGHT

Ewing decided to strike at the Hessians after dark. On the night of December 21, 1776, his men blackened their faces. They were harder to spot that way. Then they quietly rowed across the Delaware.

Ewing's team set fire to the buildings at the ferry landing. They worked quickly. Then they left as fast as they came.

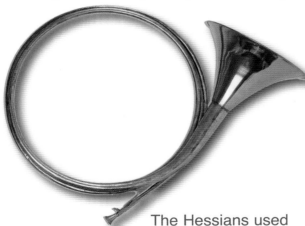

The Hessians used brass horns to call their troops to battle.

The Hessians were shaken. From then on, they all slept in their uniforms. They had to be ready for an attack at any time.

The raids especially pleased Washington. He had hoped to upset the Hessians. It

George Washington (at right) was pleased with James Ewing's raids on the Hessians.

would be easier to fight worn-out soldiers than well-rested ones.

Some of Washington's men now urged him to act. They were ready to strike at Trenton. They wanted to make a major attack.

WHAT WOULD YOU DO?

What if you were Washington? *Would you . . .*

* **Attack the Hessians now? Once the enemy gets enough boats, they could attack you.**

* **Wait for more supplies to come? Some of your men do not even have boots.**

* **Try to hold off until spring? Getting across the river would be easier once the large chunks of ice melted.**

WASHINGTON PLANS AN ATTACK

Washington planned a large-scale attack for Christmas night. He knew the Hessians would not expect a holiday attack. He also thought that the Hessians might be tired and drunk after celebrating all day.

If Washington won at Trenton, it would mean a lot to his men. Yet it would not be easy. As

A messenger gives Colonel Rall a note describing Washington's plan to attack.

Hessian soldiers (like the one at the right) knew that the Americans planned to attack. They kept an eye out for Washington's troops.

it turned out, the British leaders learned of Washington's plans. They warned Rall.

On other Christmas days, the Hessian soldiers celebrated and relaxed. This year, they remained on guard.

It was not a very merry Christmas. The Hessians were tired and discouraged. Many longed for a good night's sleep.

WHAT WOULD YOU DO?

What if you were a British leader? *Would you . . .*

* **Send more soldiers to the area? You cannot spare many soldiers, but now you need every man at Trenton.**

* **Order Rall to get his men out of Trenton fast? Let the enemy find an empty camp.**

* **Let Rall handle this? The Continental Army should be easy to defeat.**

HESSIANS DEFEND TRENTON ALONE

Rall was left to defend Trenton alone. The British leaders were sure the battle would be short. They expected a quick and easy victory.

On Christmas Day, Rall posted one hundred soldiers around the town. Others took turns patrolling the area. The tired soldiers did not rest until nightfall.

Hessian soldiers stood guard throughout the town of Trenton.

24

A winter storm raged the night that Washington planned to attack.

Then a very bad winter storm struck. At that point, the soldiers finally stopped their nighttime patrols. The Hessians did not think General Washington could attack in such bad weather.

WHAT WOULD YOU DO?

What if you were a Hessian officer in Trenton? *Would you . . .*

✱ **Cancel the next day's pre-dawn patrol? That would give your men a chance to rest. On the other hand, what if Washington made a bold attack in the storm?**

HESSIAN PATROLS ARE CALLED OFF

The Hessian officers called off the early patrol. Everyone thought they were safe now.

Washington wanted to attack Trenton before dawn.

Washington did not want to let the weather stop him. He was determined to catch the Hessians off guard. He wanted to strike before daylight.

Yet by nightfall, the snow fell harder. The winds were worse too. Ice chunks closed off parts of the river.

The boats of Washington's army would have to carry soldiers, weapons, and ammunition. Above, an actor playing a colonial soldier stands near the type of river boat used during the Revolutionary War.

Washington had more to take across the river than just soldiers. He needed horses, cannons, and ammunition too. The trip across the Delaware would be both difficult and dangerous.

Washington's men were to be joined by two other units from his army. One of these was a large group led by James Ewing. Ewing had successfully raided the Hessians in the past. Now his men, along with another unit, could not get

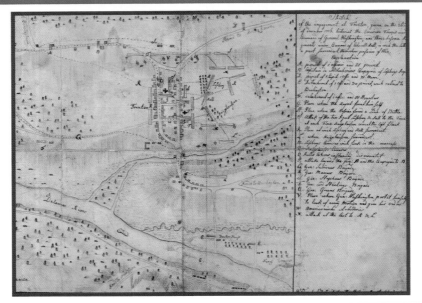

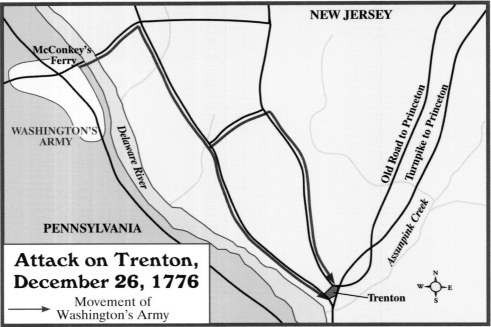

Attack on Trenton, December 26, 1776

→ Movement of Washington's Army

A plan for the Battle of Trenton (top) was made by Lieutenant Von Kraft. In order to attack Trenton, George Washington's army would not only have to cross the icy Delaware River. It also would have to march for miles in the snow.

across the river. A huge ice jam in the river blocked their crossing point.

The men were unable to move their boats. So they could not cross at another point either. That meant Washington would be short of men.

His own troops still had to cross the river in a storm. After that they had to march nine miles to reach the Hessian camp at Trenton. Many of the men would be walking through the snow without boots.

Washington thought hard about what lay ahead.

WHAT WOULD YOU DO?

If you were Washington, *would you* . . .

* Go ahead with your attack plan?

* Wait a few days until the ice jam melts? That way the other soldiers could join you.

* Call off the main attack until spring? Have Ewing keep up the raids until then. This will further weaken the enemy.

WASHINGTON LEADS AN ATTACK

Washington went ahead with the attack. He had hoped to strike before dawn. Yet by the time his soldiers got to Trenton, it was already daylight.

Washington then divided his men into two groups. One group struck from the west. The other attacked from the town's north.

Washington leads his troops to their boats as they begin crossing the Delaware River to attack Trenton.

General George Washington crosses the Delaware River. This painting was done by Emanuel Leutze in 1851. In real life, the waters of the Delaware River would have probably been too rough for Washington to stand up in the boat.

Despite the daylight, the Hessians were still surprised to see the Americans. The Hessians were caught in the center of town. Colonel Rall spotted Washington with his men on some high ground to the north. Rall told his men to get the cannons. He ordered them to fire directly on Washington and his men.

After crossing the Delaware, Washington and his soldiers faced a long march to Trenton.

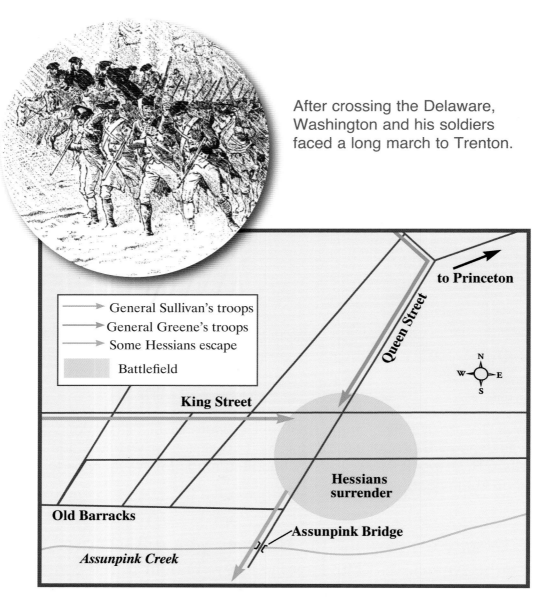

General Sullivan's troops
General Greene's troops
Some Hessians escape
Battlefield

to Princeton

Queen Street

King Street

N
W   E
S

Hessians surrender

Old Barracks

Assunpink Bridge

Assunpink Creek

Washington had American generals Greene and Sullivan attack the Hessians from two different directions. While most of the Hessians ended up being killed or captured, some escaped across Assunpink Bridge.

Washington's men fired back with their cannons. Eight Hessian gunners were killed. The other gunners quickly fled.

Colonel Rall led his men out of the line of fire to an apple orchard on the outskirts of town. From there, he turned his men north. He still hoped to bring down Washington's troops on the high ground.

However, just then, Rall was given some bad news. He learned that his gunners had deserted two of their cannons. The men had run under fire.

Rall saw this as a blow to his honor as a leader. He felt that his entire unit had been shamed.

WHAT WOULD YOU DO?

What if you were Colonel Rall? *Would you . . .*

* Go to the town's center and try to take back the cannons?

* Put aside your pride and just do your best to win the battle?

RALL GOES BACK FOR THE CANNONS

Rall led his men into the center of town. He hoped to take back the cannons. He succeeded but not for long. The colonists soon seized the big guns and turned them on the Hessians.

From that point, things went badly for the Hessians. They lost twenty-two men. Colonel Rall was wounded and eventually died

The Americans fought bravely at the Battle of Trenton.

Rall was wounded during the battle. Soon after he surrendered, the Hessian colonel died of his injuries.

from his injury. The Hessians knew they could not win. Before he died, Rall surrendered to Washington.

Washington and his men finally had the victory they longed for. Amazingly, no Americans were killed in the fight. Washington wrote to Congress noting that "only two officers and one or two privates [were] wounded."

Yet Washington's problems were not over. In many cases, the time his men were required to be soldiers was

Some of the Hessian soldiers escaped across a bridge over Assunpink Creek.

nearly up. They could leave the army and go home if they wished.

These men were tired and cold. They still had few warm clothes to wear and only a couple of blankets. More than a few had no boots. On the march to Trenton, some had left bloody footprints in the snow.

Others had fallen into the icy Delaware River during the crossing. They had to be fished out of the cold water.

Cold and weary soldiers of the Continental Army warm themselves around an open fire. Many of them had to decide whether to continue fighting.

These men had to stay in freezing weather wearing damp clothes. Many had good reason to want a long rest away from the army.

However, Washington needed a large army to win the war. He asked his men to stay. He told them that their new country's future depended on them.

WHAT WOULD YOU DO?

What if you were a soldier? *Would you . . .*

✳ **Leave?**

✳ **Stay to fight with General Washington?**

WASHINGTON'S MEN STAY

Most of the men stayed. After winning at Trenton, they had a new sense of pride. Washington planned his next move.

He knew that there were many British soldiers at the nearby town of Princeton. Soon word of the Hessian defeat at Trenton would reach them. Washington guessed that they would attack then.

This musket was used by Hessian troops during the Revolutionary War.

Most of Washington's soldiers stayed in the Continental Army. They were proud of their victory.

Lieutenant General Charles Cornwallis (above) was leading an army of British and Hessian soldiers toward Washington's camp.

He was right. By January 2, a force of both British and Hessian soldiers was on its way. It was led by British Lieutenant General Charles Cornwallis.

Washington sent out some men to try to hold them off. However, they were not very successful. Cornwallis soon neared Washington's camp. His men were ready for battle. They planned to strike the next morning.

WHAT WOULD YOU DO?

What if you were Washington? *Would you . . .*

* Stand your ground and fight? You just had a victory in Trenton. You could win again.

* Quickly go back across the Delaware? The British still do not have enough boats to come after you.

* Quietly sneak away from the camp after dark? Take most of your men with you. Go to Princeton and try to take that town. Many of the men that were protecting Princeton are here with Cornwallis.

WASHINGTON ATTACKS PRINCETON

Washington decided to try for another victory. He and his men left for Princeton before dawn. Later that morning, Cornwallis arrived at their empty camp. He came ready to fight and found them all gone.

The Americans did their fighting at Princeton that day. Some were killed, and others were wounded. Yet within hours, they won the battle.

George Washington's crossing of the Delaware is honored on the back of the New Jersey state quarter.

The Americans were victorious at the Battle of Princeton.

The victories at Trenton and Princeton were important. Americans again believed that their army could help them win their independence. From there, Washington and his men took back much of New Jersey from the British.

The fight for independence would go on for years. There were some defeats. However, the Americans won important victories at Sarasota, New York, in October 1777 and at Cowpens, South Carolina, in January 1781.

Cornwallis later surrendered at Yorktown, Virginia, in 1781. This was the end of the Revolutionary War. The United States was free from British rule.

Then in October 1783, General Cornwallis surrendered at Yorktown. That was the last major battle of the war. By then, many Americans had died fighting. Yet it was the price these soldiers were willing to pay. Today Americans live in the free and independent nation for which these men fought and died.

TIMELINE

1776—Early December: The Continental army is camped in Pennsylvania near the banks of the Delaware River.
December 17: James Ewing and his men raid the Hessian outpost at Trenton, New Jersey
December 18: Ewing and his men raid the Hessian outpost at Trenton a second time.
December 21: Ewing and his men make their first nighttime raid on the Hessian outpost at Trenton.
December 26: Washington and his men defeat the Hessians at the Battle of Trenton.

1777—January 2: General Charles Cornwallis leads a force of British and Hessian soldiers toward Washington's camp near Trenton.
January 3: The Continental army wins the Battle of Princeton in New Jersey.
October 17: The Continental army defeats the British at the Battle of Saratoga in New York.

1781—January 17: The Continental army wins the Battle of Cowpens in South Carolina.

1783—October 19: British General Charles Cornwallis surrenders at Yorktown in the last major battle of the American Revolution; Americans win their independence.

WORDS TO KNOW

ammunition—Things fired from weapons, such as cannonballs or bullets.

barricade—A wall or fence to block people from getting past.

Continental Army—The colonists' fighting force during the American Revolution.

ferry—A boat that carries people across water.

gunner—A person trained to fire a cannon.

Hessian—A person from a certain area of Germany.

historian—Someone who studies history.

ice jam—A block caused by large chunks of ice in a stretch of water.

outpost—A military camp away from where the bulk of the soldiers are.

pre-dawn—Very early in the morning; before dawn.

recruit—Getting someone to join an army; someone who joins an army.

retreat—To move back or away from a battle.

seized—Taken by force.

surrender—To give up.

Learn More

Books

Armentrout, David. George Washington. Vero Beach, Fla.: Rourke Publications, 2004.

Cheney, Lynne. When Washington Crossed the Delaware. New York: Simon & Schuster, 2004.

Doeden, Matt. George Washington: Heading a New Nation. Mankato, Minn.: Capstone Press, 2006.

Farshtey, Greg. The American Revolution. San Diego, Calif.: Kidhaven Press, 2003.

Stewart, Gail. The American Revolution. San Diego, Calif.: Blackbirch Press, 2004.

Internet Addresses

The American Revolution

<www.theamericanrevolution.org>

Check out this Web site to learn all about the colonists' fight for freedom. Don't miss the link on battles. You will see how the colonists won the war!

The George Washington Papers

<http://gwpapers.virginia.edu/education/kids/kids1.html>

This Web site has lots of information on how George Washington crossed the Delaware. You can learn more about Washington here as well.

INDEX